From a Sinner to a Saint
Discerning Your Spiritual Seasons
Workbook

Danielle Johnson

Book Cover Design: Michelle Stimpson

Printed by Prize Publishing House, LLC
in the United States of America.

First printing edition 2025.

Prize Publishing House
P.O. Box 9856, Chesapeake, VA 23321
www.PrizePublishingHouse.com

ISBN (Paperback): 979-8-9925617-5-3

This workbook was designed from Chapter 5 in my book "From a Sinner to a Saint." If you haven't gotten a copy, I recommend that you would read that before tackling the workbook. This workbook will help give you a better understanding of what spiritual season you are in and how to best handle each season. As I was going through my transition from smoking marijuana and amongst other things, understanding my spiritual seasons really helped me deal with all the trials that I was facing. We know that trials will come to make us stronger, but they can be overwhelming at times. I always say that when you know what you are fighting and how to fight it then you can overcome everything that comes against you.

As I stated in my book From a Sinner to as Saint, I started to separate myself from everything and put my focus on God. The enemy will try to use our busy lives to distract us from the plan that God has laid out for us and when the light bulb went off for me, my desire of wanting more burned so deep, that I knew I had to begin the journey of changing my ways. One day during my time of prayer, the Holy Spirit told me that I needed to be delivered from myself. That shocked me to say the least. I was like "delivered from myself?"

We always ask God to deliver us from whatever we are dealing with or facing at that particular moment. But we never ask Him to deliver us from us. I mean just think about it, sometimes we can be our own worst enemies. We would hinder ourselves from receiving what God has for us, by choosing to hold on to strongholds that should be easy to let go. I'm realizing that for me to be set free from anything that is holding me captive, then I have to get out of the way and let God be God.

Look I get it, it's hard but if you put forth the effort then God will do the rest. So today I challenge you to take that first step towards deliverance by asking the Holy Spirit to DELIVER YOU FROM YOU! Now is the time to take back YOU...

In the book, I discuss six seasons or areas in our lives that God will like to bring to our awareness so that we can be a powerful force in His kingdom. Each week will begin a new season for you to focus on and an area to write down what the Spirit lays upon your heart concerning that season and week.

Season 1 (Week 1): Developing Your Heart

Grow or cause to grow and become more mature, advanced, or elaborate

In order to receive the Word of God you must first prepare the ground of your heart, Jeremiah 17:9-10 states; "the human heart is the most deceitful of all things, and desperately wicked. Who really knows how bad it is? But I, the LORD, search all hearts and examine secret motives. I give all people their due rewards, according to what their actions deserve."

Being that man cannot trust his own heart, he must leave it all to the Father who knows the heart and judges every man fairly and that those who have a redeemed heart are the only ones who can live in a proper fellowship with the Father. If we want a changed life, we must first remove things out of our hearts that hinders the Father from entering our lives.

The Lord should be the only person sitting on the throne of our hearts. Yes, it's okay to love your spouse, children, job or whatever else that's of importance, but the Father should always come first. However, we tend to put everything before Him and when all else fails that's when we want to turn to Him. God should be the first one we run to no matter the circumstances, good or bad. I know at times things may not be peachy and cream, but we still must continue to trust God.

In our walk with the Lord we must see things as He sees them, to Him it's not what goes in us, but what more so of what we say. In Mark 7:20-23, Jesus stated, "it is what comes from inside that defiles you. For from within, out of a person's heart, come evil thoughts, sexual immorality, theft, murder, adultery, greed, wickedness, deceit, lustful desires, envy, slander, pride, and foolishness. All these vile things come from within, they are what defile you."

This is one of the reasons why we should make sure that our heart is pure, if it's filled with evil, then evil is what will come out, but if you fill it with good things, then good things are what you will release. Like the Bible says, a good person produces good things from the treasury of a good heart, and an evil person produces evil things from the treasury of an evil heart. What you say flows from what is in your heart." (Luke 6:45)

Everything we speak into the atmosphere should align up with the word of God. When I decided to get saved, this was one of the most important things I had to do. As I stated in the book, one of the steps I took to prepare my heart was making sure I attended weekly bible study and applied what I learned to my life. When you are being taught the Word and choose not to act on it, you are unable to experience the blessings that come with obedience. How would you know if God is a healer if you never applied his word of healing to your life? How would you know if he's a way maker if you have never applied his word of being Jehovah Jireh to your life? God says to try the Spirit by the spirit. And to keep it honest, I'm still learning to do this.

For this week's lesson, I want you to take some time and examine your heart and ask yourself these questions and give yourself some time to ponder over them before answering.

1. If you could see a visual of your heart what would it look like?

_____

_____

_____

_____

_____

_____

_____

_____

_____

_____

_____

_____

_____

_____

_____

_____

2. What strongholds am I holding on too that's causing me to not move forward in my life?

_____

_____

_____

_____

_____

_____

_____

_____

_____

_____

_____

_____

_____

_____

_____

_____

_____

_____

3. What are you carrying in your heart (i.e. unforgiveness, bitterness, hurt, pain or jealousy, etc.)?

_____

_____

_____

_____

_____

_____

_____

_____

_____

_____

_____

_____

_____

_____

_____

_____

_____

4. The state that your heart is in right now, do you think God is pleased?

_____

_____

_____

_____

_____

_____

_____

_____

_____

_____

_____

_____

_____

_____

_____

_____

_____

_____

Season 2 (Week 2): Inserting the Seed

Place in the ground so it can grow

When it comes to God's Word, it is important that it is planted on a ground that is nurtured. When we nurture God's Word, we are letting Him know that we not only care for his Word but that we also cherish it. Our desire is for His Word to become active in our lives. It is one thing to hear something that can help you, but it's something different when you apply what you have heard to your life.

To some of us, and this includes believers, sowing can be a mystery. When we give something away, it comes back to us like a boomerang. However, that is a concept that some of us still haven't grabbed hold too yet. We will look at our bills and think, "how can I sow this $100 dollar and my light bill is due?" You cannot expect change when you are not willing to apply the change to your lives. Change can only come by doing something.

A sower is a person who plants something as a lifestyle no matter what they are faced with. Throughout my walk, with Christ, I would not allow my circumstances to rule over me. I had to make sure that whatever I sowed would reap a harvest and that everything I planted was inserted into good soil. God will give you more seeds to sow when you sow what you have into good ground. I have come to learn that my harvest will not come from tithes but my offering. What I give!

Remember, when you are following the Kingdom principle than you will be blessed. "But don't just listen to God's word. You must do what it is says. Otherwise, you are only fooling yourselves. (James 1:22)

When we plant something, we expect it to grow. For this reason, God wants us to be careful with the words we speak in our lives and in the lives of others.

For this week's lesson, think about all the seeds you have planted, whether good or bad. Ask yourself these questions and give yourself some time to ponder over them before answering.

1. What seeds did you allow to be planted in your spirit?

_____

_____

_____

_____

_____

_____

_____

_____

_____

_____

_____

_____

_____

_____

_____

_____

_____

2. Were they good or bad seeds?

_____

_____

_____

_____

_____

_____

_____

_____

_____

_____

_____

_____

_____

_____

_____

_____

3. Did they come in the form of a thought or a word either from you or someone else?

_____

_____

_____

_____

_____

_____

_____

_____

_____

_____

_____

_____

_____

_____

_____

_____

_____

_____

4. How did you handle it?

_____

_____

_____

_____

_____

_____

_____

_____

_____

_____

_____

_____

_____

_____

_____

_____

Season 3 (Week 3): Scattering the Seeds

Throw in various random directions

The process of fertilizing a substance is to increase the growth of that substance. As we mature in life there should always be some evidence of growth in your life, whether it's the way that you think, talk or react to things. When it comes to Gods word, you should see a level of maturity in your life, especially when you apply it to your life.

Once you have received the word, you must guard your heart and that word. This season is the season when the enemy throws any and everything at you to make you lose focus. He will use strangers, friends and even family to get under your skin. His job is to make you lose the Word that was just planted in your spirit.

Let's look at this through the eyes of a farmer. When a farmer fertilizes the soil, his objective is to make sure that the seeds that were planted will grow. To do this, he must toil the ground and nurture it so that the seeds can be planted on fertile ground. That is how it should be when it comes to the Word of God. The enemy will try to cloud your mind with so many negative things to make you doubt God's Word. His sole purpose is to blind your mind, it is important for us to know that the powers of evil are helpless to do anything unless they first have gained ground to man's will, emotions and body.

If you allow the enemy to take control of your mind, he has you, he can work freely without asking for an invitation.

After I got out of that relationship with the married guy, I remember being in prayer one night and the enemy said to me, "he does not hear you. Look what you did, I don't know why you are on your knees, you might as well get up." And just like that, I would stop praying. See, the enemy planted negative thoughts in my mind. He didn't want me to ask for forgiveness let alone be forgiving.

The enemy's goal is to distract you and keep you from being in fellowship with God. He wanted me to believe that God no longer loved me and that I wasn't forgiven. But God said in Romans 8:1, "So now there is no condemnation for those who belong to Christ Jesus" So, when those thoughts of doubt, fear, worry or self-loath come; your job is to cast down those imaginations (2 Corinthians 10:5). I once heard someone say, "the birds can fly over your head, but they don't have to nest there." Basically, the thoughts are going to come, but you don't have to let it stay. We must trust God, rest in His Word, and bind and cast out those toxic thoughts!

For this week's lesson, ask yourself these questions and give yourself some time to ponder over them before answering.

1. Did the enemy use those closes to you?

_____

_____

_____

_____

_____

_____

_____

_____

_____

_____

_____

_____

_____

_____

_____

_____

_____

2. Who were they?

_____

_____

_____

_____

_____

_____

_____

_____

_____

_____

_____

_____

_____

_____

_____

_____

_____

_____

3. How did you handle the situation?

_____

_____

_____

_____

_____

_____

_____

_____

_____

_____

_____

_____

_____

_____

_____

_____

_____

4. And did you forgive those that were a part of the situation or have you allowed yourself to be forgiven?

_____

_____

_____

_____

_____

_____

_____

_____

_____

_____

_____

_____

_____

_____

_____

_____

_____

Season 4 (Week 4): Saturate the Seed

Cause (something) to become thoroughly soaked with liquid so that no more can be absorbed

This is the season when you must pray, praise, worship, and confess God's Word daily. Prayer is your life line to God and when you pray, you are joining forces with God. You should get into a place in your life where all you do is put a praise on everything. I don't care how bad it looks… PRAISE! I don't care how good it feels… PRAISE! Remember it's not about you and your feelings, it's about God getting the Glory out of your life. And for Him to do that you must praise your way out. I remind myself of this daily. In my book to describe this season, I gave a parable of a farmer, when a farmer plant seeds, their objective is to grow their crops in hopes of reaping a harvest. Farmers must know what nutrients are needed. They are up early watering their crops, and they are faithful to this task. If we look at our relationship with God in the same manner, we can see where we are and how much more we can do to draw closer to Him.

The seed that is planted into our spirits should be watered daily. Basically, it's time for us to have a mindset like a farmer. "O God, you are my God; I earnestly search for you. My soul thirsts for you; my whole body longs for you in this parched and weary land where there is no water." (Psalm 63:1-3)

Even though hardships may come, we must remember that they have come to make us stronger, they have come to test our faith and most importantly, the hardships have come to pass. God is still in it with you. He said He'll never leave us nor will He forsake us and that is why it is very important that we understand the power of praise and worship. Believe it or not, along with giving, it is your praise that has taken you this far, it will be your praise that will bring you out and it will be your praise that will bring you into your harvest.

A seed can consist of many things and it can be good or bad. So, for this week's lesson, ask yourself these questions and give yourself some time to ponder over them before answering.

1. How important is saturating your seeds are too you?

_____

_____

_____

_____

_____

_____

_____

_____

_____

_____

_____

_____

_____

_____

_____

_____

_____

_____

2. What methods do you take to saturate your seed?

_____

_____

_____

_____

_____

_____

_____

_____

_____

_____

_____

_____

_____

_____

_____

_____

_____

_____

3. Were you consistent with it?

_____

_____

_____

_____

_____

_____

_____

_____

_____

_____

_____

_____

_____

_____

_____

_____

_____

4. Can you do more to be effective in your season of saturating your seeds?

_____

_____

_____

_____

_____

_____

_____

_____

_____

_____

_____

_____

_____

_____

_____

_____

_____

_____

Season 5 (Week 5): Removing the Weeds

Eliminate or get rid of

This is one of the seasons that's hard if not challenging for some of us. I know it was for me, to be honest sometimes it still is. Weeding out the weeds is when we allow God to remove things or individuals out of our lives that mean us no good. Note I stated, "allow God to remove," this is where we tend to get in the way of God. I know this is something I did faithfully. And when that happens, we hinder our growth and block our blessings.

Weeds are made to choke what is growing. Imagine you have a garden where you're planting the most beautiful flowers. One day you notice there are weeds in your flower bed. What do you do? Like any gardener, your first reaction is to pluck the weeds up to keep them from destroying the flowers.

Weeds are ugly and very undesirable. If we look at our lives, we can see individuals or habits that are ugly and undesirable to God; those things or people are there only to choke what has been planted in our hearts.

When I began to take my walk seriously, God started removing people out of my life. When the removing and separation of people started to happen, I was scared; these were people that I knew for a long time, I considered them to be good friends. However, to God, it was time to weed out the weeds. I had to be extremely careful about what I "ate." I had to guard my heart because the enemy was angry, and he would test me just to find out what I knew. We must understand the process we are in because the enemy will try to keep you out of the will of God.

As believers, we should always do a spiritual inventory and check our lives. Who is in our spiritual house illegally? Who or what is God trying to remove that is occupying the spot where the Holy Spirit should be? Then begin eliminating everything and everyone out of your life that goes against your faith and hinders your call. Weed out those undesirable weeds by renewing your mind and casting out those seeds by suffocating the enemy with the Word of God.

Some of us tend to think we know what's best so we try to rationalize why these habits or people should remain, but only the Father knows what's best for us. God tells us in Jeremiah 29:11, "For I know the plans I have for you," says the LORD. "They are plans for good and not for disaster, to give you a future and a hope." Just step aside and let God do what He does best. For this week's lesson, ask yourself these questions and give yourself some time to ponder over them before answering.

1. Are there any weeds in your life that needs to be uprooted?

_____

_____

_____

_____

_____

_____

_____

_____

_____

_____

_____

_____

_____

_____

_____

_____

_____

_____

_____

2. How did you recognize those weeds?

_____

_____

_____

_____

_____

_____

_____

_____

_____

_____

_____

_____

_____

_____

_____

_____

_____

_____

3. What steps did you take to uproot those weeds?

_____

_____

_____

_____

_____

_____

_____

_____

_____

_____

_____

_____

_____

_____

_____

_____

_____

_____

_____

4. How did you feel once you begin to remove those weeds from your life?

_____

_____

_____

_____

_____

_____

_____

_____

_____

_____

_____

_____

_____

_____

_____

_____

_____

_____

Season 6 (Week 6): Season of Reaping

Receive (a reward or benefit) as a consequence of one's own or other people's actions

I don't know about you, but after going through those first five seasons, this is the one I have been waiting for…the season of harvest. The season of harvest is for those that have allowed their hearts to be prepared, the seed to be planted, it to be watered, the ground to be fertilized and the weeds to be removed. A farmer knows that there will be a reward at the end of his planting, especially if he has been taking care of the soil like he should. This is how it is with God when we do what is required.

God promised us that we will have plentiful and live a life of abundance that we wouldn't have room enough to receive. In this season, I couldn't be lazy, I had to be steadfast and diligent. I couldn't listen to the ungodly or those that couldn't give a word of encouragement. What I mean by this is when you are working in your season of harvest, those that do not understand it will speak negativity into your spirit and try to discourage you. I am sure you have heard someone say, "Why you trying to go back to school at your age?" When those kinds of questions come at you, I need for you to do three things; One, do not listen to those negative people, they just want you to be as miserable as they are. Two, rebuke that devil right in his face. And three, go hard and prove that devil wrong. Please understand, I am not calling the individual the devil. But let's be real, the enemy will use anybody to get you off track including those closest to you to make you lose focus. So, to sum this part up, don't fall for the devil's tricks. Stay the course and soar like the eagle that you are and called to be.

Another reason I love this season is that it lets us know that there is an expiration date on what we are facing. So, if we persevere just a little bit longer, push one more time, praise a little louder, and trust a bit more; we will reap, if we faint not. Paul proclaimed to the Galatians, "So let's not get tired of doing what is good. At just the right time we will reap a harvest of blessing if we don't give up" (Galatians 6:9). As I stated before, if you take hold of these seasons, begin to understand what season you are in and apply them to your life, not only will they bless you, but you will have a greater understanding on how to bind the enemy. During your season of harvest, you still have work to do. Reaping a harvest is not only about your return. It is also about what you are depositing into your harvest, which is extremely important. The devil will use people for a season to make you miss your season. Let me say that again, the devil will use people for a season to make you miss your season.

During this season YOU CANNOT BECOME DISTRACTED!

Ask yourself these questions on what you feel can help you remain strong and undistracted in your season of harvest. Give yourself some time to ponder over them before answering.

1. Are there any thing or someone in your life that may be a distraction to you? (social media, family, friends or work)

_____
_____
_____
_____
_____
_____
_____
_____
_____
_____
_____
_____
_____
_____
_____
_____
_____
_____

2. Are the distractions easier or harder to remove now that you have become aware of them?

_____

_____

_____

_____

_____

_____

_____

_____

_____

_____

_____

_____

_____

_____

_____

_____

_____

3. What steps are you taking to remove those distractions?

4. Have you notice any positive changes since eliminating these distractions?

_____

_____

_____

_____

_____

_____

_____

_____

_____

_____

_____

_____

_____

_____

_____

_____

_____

About The Author

Danielle Johnson is a mom. Her favorite scripture is Jeremiah 29:11. She graduated from Tidewater Community College in 2013 with her Associates of Applied Science Degree in Management. She will be graduating in May 2023 from Regent University with her Bachelor's Degree in Professional Studies with a concentration in Teacher Education.

She has written two children's books titled Chubb the Chipmunk and Ashley Nalayla goes to the Nail Salon. She is a featured author in an anthology titled Love Hope Faith. As an author, her goal is to minister to as many readers as possible through her writing. Her desire is for readers to feel the authenticity of her story while making a difference in their lives. She hopes that the words she shares on each page reaches their hearts and are not looked at as mere words on paper, but that they feel her heart beat through her words.

Danielle's desire is for her readers to be able to see themselves in the text, and prayerfully through the Holy Spirit, be delivered and set free. Her mission to accomplish her desires with reaching her readers is through being transparent, realistic and relatable. She wants to use her testimony as a platform to minister and help women who are broken in their spirit.

For I know the plans I have for you," says the Lord. "They are plans for good and not for disaster, to give you a future and a hope. Jeremiah 29:11